CARTOON TIPS

Learn to draw your own brilliant cartoon characters

Frank Rodgers

Hippo

**Look out for
ANIMAL ART
CARTOON FUN
COMIC FUN
COUNT DRAWCULA'S CARTOON FUN
also by Frank Rodgers**

Scholastic Children's Books,
Commonwealth House,
1-19 New Oxford Street,
London WC1A 1NU, UK
A division of Scholastic Ltd
London ~ New York ~ Toronto ~ Sydney ~ Auckland

First published by Scholastic Ltd, 1997

Copyright © Frank Rodgers, 1997

ISBN 0 590 19853 X

Printed in Spain by G.Z. Printek

10 8 6 4 2 1 3 5 7 9

Contents

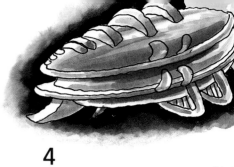

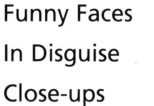

Funny Faces

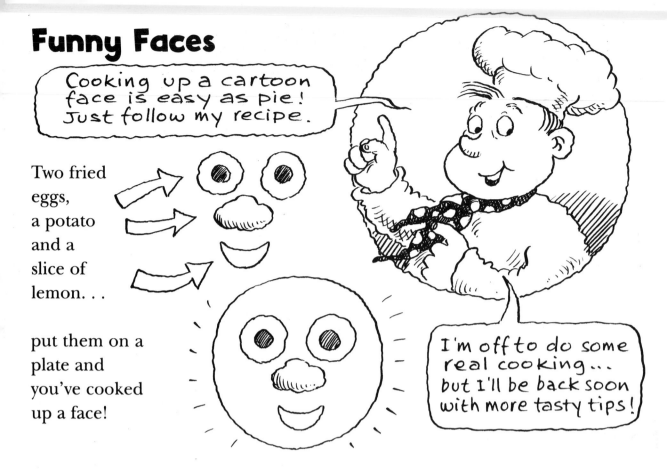

Cooking up a cartoon face is easy as pie! Just follow my recipe.

Two fried eggs, a potato and a slice of lemon. . .

put them on a plate and you've cooked up a face!

I'm off to do some real cooking. . . but I'll be back soon with more tasty tips!

If the cartoon chef's method is not to your taste then try this. Take the same ingredients. . . I mean features. . . of eyes, nose and mouth and put them on another plate. . . sorry, I mean put another outline round them. . . like this.

The eyes don't have to look like fried eggs, of course, they can look like this. . .

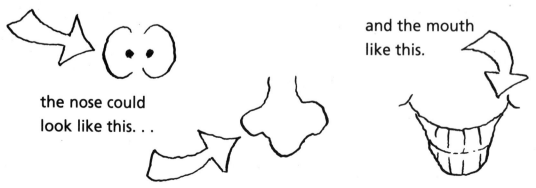

the nose could look like this. . .

and the mouth like this.

4

Put them all together
and add a head shape,
and this is what you get.

Or, change the
nose. . .

and turn it
into an animal!

Stretchy Bodies

The basic
cartoon body
shape looks
like this. . .

but look what
you can do if
you stretch it. . .

and knead
it. . . like a
lump of dough!

In Disguise

Using hats and glasses is a great way to make your funny face even funnier.

Or try changing the hairstyle!

Guess who?

Disguising your cartoon character in different clothes is fun too!

Close-ups

Cartoon faces don't have to be simple. . . they can be as detailed or as complicated as you like.

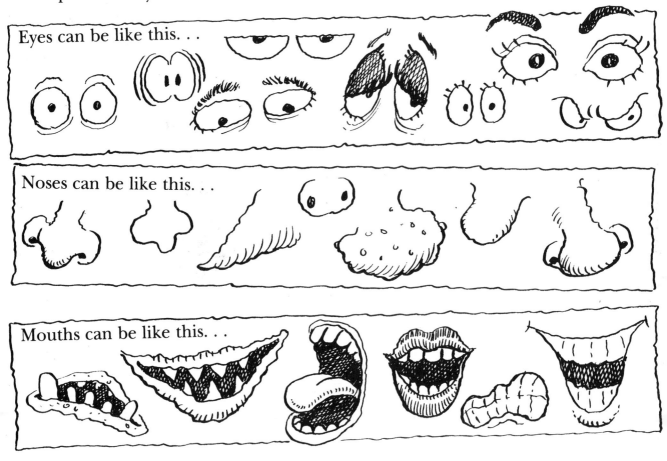

Eyes can be like this. . .

Noses can be like this. . .

Mouths can be like this. . .

If you are drawing eyes from the side and want to make them look more realistic, just imagine the shape of the eyeball. . . and draw the eyelids over it.

Eyeball

pupil

Top eyelid

Bottom eyelid

From the side, noses and mouths look like this.

Put them together to create cartoon profiles, then add the rest of the head and some details.

Profiles and turning heads are easy peasy if you follow the instructions below. By the way, I've got a pretty good profile, don't you think?

Draw an oval shape. . .

then add an extra line at the bottom.

Draw the face using the lower guide-line for the mouth and chin.

Draw the head shape again and put in the guide-lines for the eyes and the nose.

Then add the extra guide-line again at the bottom. . .

and finish it off by drawing the features like this.

In a three-quarter view like this you see a bit more of the face as it turns towards you.

3D Effects

To achieve a solid (3D) effect on a figure or an object you must first of all decide where the light is coming from. For instance, if the light comes from the left, then all the shadows will be on the right. . . like this.

Start with simple objects like a ball, a tube and a box. Mix three tones of whatever colour you are going to use. Make them light, medium and dark.

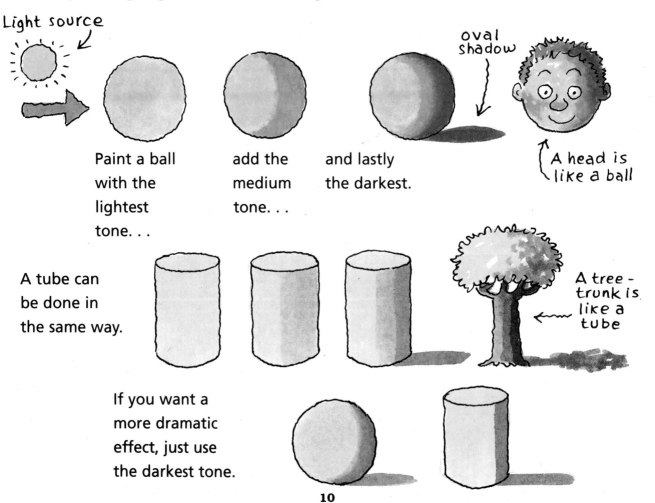

Light source

Paint a ball with the lightest tone. . .

add the medium tone. . .

and lastly the darkest.

oval shadow

A head is like a ball

A tube can be done in the same way.

A tree - trunk is like a tube

If you want a more dramatic effect, just use the darkest tone.

The shadow of a box can be done like this.

Light source

This side dark
This side not so dark

This side light

A car can be like three boxes stuck together

This is my face with the light shining right on it.

Shadows on both sides

Look what happens when the light comes from this side.

Shadow curves round the hat

Shadows curve round the forehead, nose, cheek and chin.

shadows on one side

When you are painting shadows on a figure, just imagine it's made up of boxes, tubes and a ball. . . like this.

Then paint your cartoon figure.

Animals can be done the same way.

What a Character!

Before you draw a character you have to think about how it looks. Work out a recipe for it in your head.

Like this!

Pirate Recipe

Take one pirate hat; one eye-patch; one scowling, bearded face; one frilly shirt; one waistband with cutlass and pistol; one hook; one wooden leg and one sea-boot. Mix together on a sheet of paper with pencil and pen.

Remember, it's a good idea to sketch in the rough shapes first. . . like this.

Hat like a slice of lemon

Round head

fat, round body

frills on shirt

Wide trousers

Buckle on shoe

Or. . .
think of a
marathon runner
and you think of
a thin muscular
body, short hair,
thin face, vest,
number, shorts
and running shoes.

Oval head
Hair like a wedge
Body like a peanut
Long, thin legs
Big feet

Think of a
monster and
you think
YEEUCH!

Eyes like frog-spawn
Body covered in fish-scales
Arms and legs like tree-trunks
Hands like bunches of bananas
talons
Big smelly feet

Think of a weight-
lifter and you think
of a small head,
wide shoulders,
barrel chest, small
waist and thick
arms and legs.

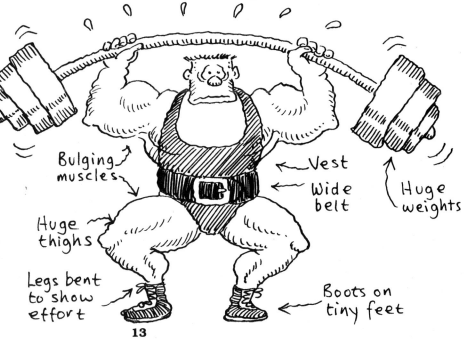

Bulging muscles
Vest
Wide belt
Huge weights
Huge thighs
Legs bent to show effort
Boots on tiny feet

13

Colourful Characters

Some cartoon characters have got colourful costumes to go with their colourful personalities!

Get out your paints or felt tips and make a list in your head of things your character would be wearing and their colours. For instance, if it was a princess, then you would probably think of these things.

Crown ⟶

Long hair

Long, triangular sleeves

Long sceptre

Broad necklace

Long, flowing cloak

Gold crown ⟶

Yellow hair

Emeralds & rubies

Golden sceptre

Royal purple cloak

White fur trim

Royal blue gown

You can use the 'list' method with any character.

Superhero

Oval head

Narrow waist

Long, muscly legs

Two contrasting bright colours

Knight

Red cross

Hair like a helmet

Oblong body

Black hair

Grey chain mail

White tunic

Brown boots

Wizard

Rainbow colours

White hair

Pointed hat

Long, pointed sleeves

Dark purple cloak

Gold stars

Silver moons

Alien

Red spikes

Pointed head

Round body

Blue skin

Short, thick legs

Green, yellow and red costume

Prehistoric Cartoons

Our earliest ancestors lived more than two million years ago and looked more like apes.

That is an insult to apes!

High eye-line

Head like a rugby ball

Forehead bulges over eyes

Low mouth-line

Small nose

Hairy face

Oval body

Long, thick arms

club like a baseball bat

Animal skin shaped like a hammock

Hairy body

Big feet

Luckily over the centuries they changed for the better. Take a look at these prehistoric pin-ups!

700,000 years ago

200,000 years ago

35,000 years ago

Round about 10,000 years ago they would have hunted animals like the woolly mammoth. . .

or they might have been hunted themselves by a sabre-tooth tiger!

Prehistoric Paintbox

Here are some methods of painting prehistoric cartoons. I've tried them all and they're as easy as pie!

The woolly mammoth can be painted like this.

First, draw the shape and paint it pale brown.

Then add dark brown with a small brush for the shading.

Finally, take a fibre-tip pen and draw in the hairy detail!

The caveman can be painted in much the same way.

The things you see when you don't have your spear!

The sabre-tooth tiger is painted like this.

Draw the shape and paint it pale beige. Leave white patches on the head and under the body.

then paint the muscle shapes using brown.

Finally, use a pen for the detail.

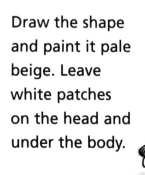

Phew! I don't think it saw me!

To create a fiery, prehistoric sky, mix these colours.

Draw a line across your paper and wet the top half with a brush dipped in clean water.

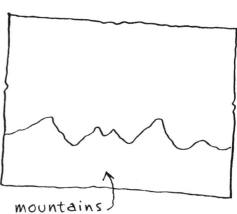

mountains

While the paper is still wet, start at the top and paint a band of purple, followed by red, orange (mix yellow and red) and yellow.

Let the colours blend

Use darker purple for the hills and darker green for the trees.

Trees painted when background is dry

The same technique can be used to paint an exploding volcano.

Draw the volcano plus the shape of the explosion.

Then start at the top of the explosion with dark purple and again add the other colours.

While the yellow is still wet, paint in red lines to create the spray effect.

Then finish off by painting the sky and the volcano.

Aliens and UFOs

What do UFOs look like?
Saucers?

Or tea-cups, perhaps?

Use your imagination. I'm sure that's what the alien spaceship builders did.

Let me cook up a design for you. First take a doughnut...

Stick an ice-cream cone on it...

Next, put on some macaroni and spaghetti...

then add as many little bits of decoration as you like!

If you look at how aliens are portrayed by actors on TV and in films you will see that they look basically human. WEIRD. . . but basically human! (It's cheaper to do this than to create electronic puppets!) Also, it's fun to mess about with the human face shape. Why don't you try it?

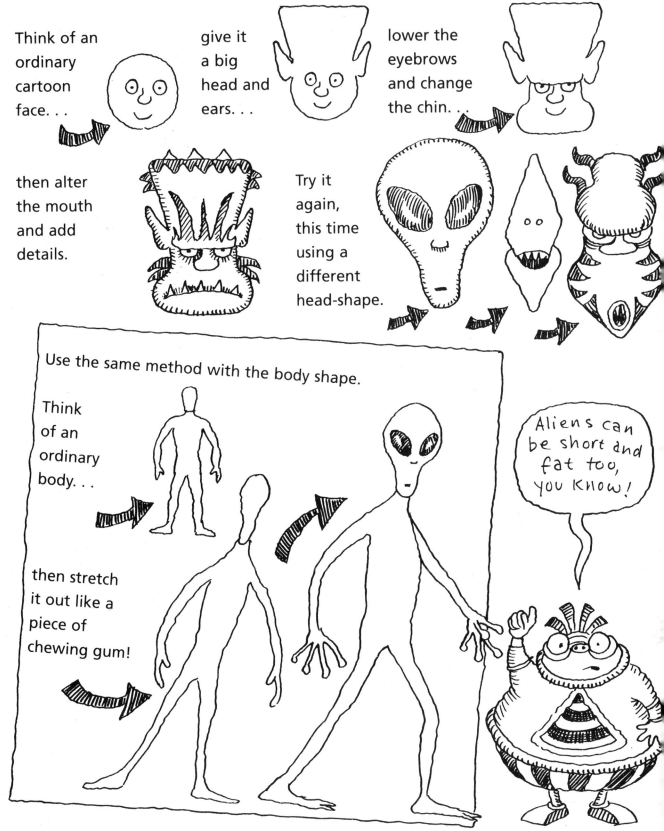

Think of an ordinary cartoon face. . .

give it a big head and ears. . .

lower the eyebrows and change the chin. . .

then alter the mouth and add details.

Try it again, this time using a different head-shape.

Use the same method with the body shape.

Think of an ordinary body. . .

then stretch it out like a piece of chewing gum!

Aliens can be short and fat too, you know!

Little Green Men?

People once imagined that Martians were little green men... but I'm sure aliens come in all shapes, sizes and colours!

Try this for a good effect.
First, draw an alien's shape on dark coloured paper.

Paint it white. While it is still wet add touches of blue and yellow. . .

to the right side of the face, body, arms and legs. Then add stars and the background.

Or, of course, you can just create your own aliens using wild, exaggerated shapes and bright colours.

When painting a spaceship in space, use a strong source of light. This will make the ship look as if it's being lit by the sun.

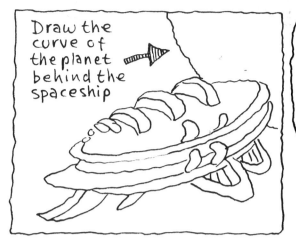

Use two tones of grey-blue for the spaceship. Paint the sky black. . .

and use bright pink and yellow for the planet and the high- lights on the spaceship.

Then, when the black sky is dry. . . paint in some planets.

Finally, add the black details of the spaceship.

Cartoon Transport

It becomes a bit more difficult when you try to draw them from an angle.

To make it easier, just imagine a car is made up of three boxes.

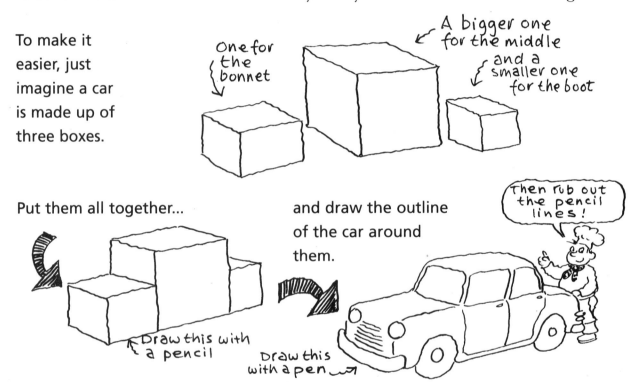

One for the bonnet

A bigger one for the middle

and a smaller one for the boot

Put them all together...

and draw the outline of the car around them.

Then rub out the pencil lines!

Draw this with a pencil

Draw this with a pen

Once you've got the hang of it you can stretch or squeeze your car into any shape!

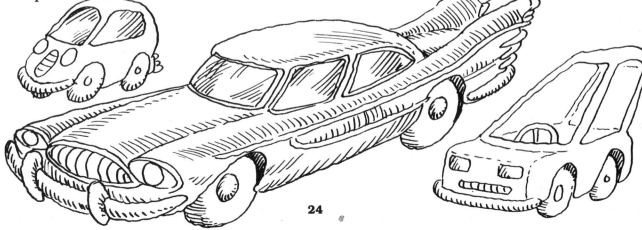

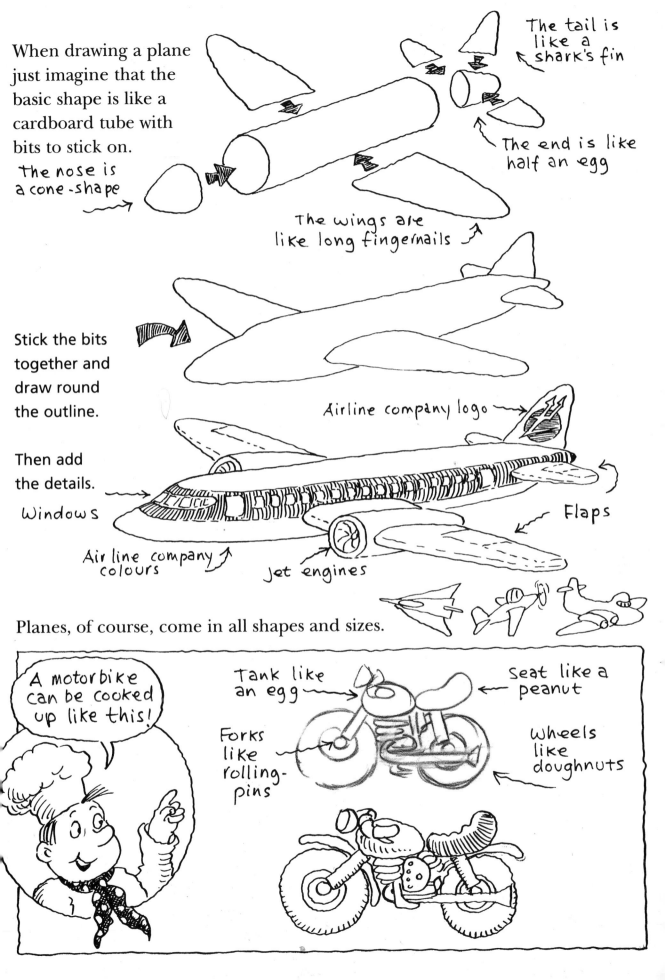

Paint Jobs

Taking a 'shine' to cartoons!

Cartoon cars can be painted 'flat' (using no shading) like this.

But if you want the car to look bright and shiny all you have to do is add reflected shapes in a darker colour.

Bus Stop

Reflection of bus stop

Look at a shiny car next time you pass and see how many objects are reflected in its shine.

Motorbikes, on the other hand, don't have a lot of shiny paintwork. . . but they do have shiny chrome!

The chrome parts can be painted like tubes. . .

but this time add another strip of tone on the opposite side.

Use this method when painting a motorbike.

26

Draw waves with foam at their tops.

Paint over the whole lot with pale green.

Then, leave the foam and paint the rest dark green.

Cartoon Cuteness

Why do people say "Ahhh," when they see a baby or a baby animal? Because they're CUTE, that's why. Here's how to draw one.

First, draw big eyes, a little nose and a smiling mouth.

A baby has a big head so add one!

Then add chubby cheeks and a small chin.

Large head

Round body

Short arms

Small hands

Short legs

Big bottom

Little feet

A baby's head is large compared to its body.

For a side-view (profile) draw the guide outline as on page 9. . .

extra line

but this time draw the eye-line much lower.

eye-line

Large forehead

little nose

mouth and chin drawn on outside guide-line

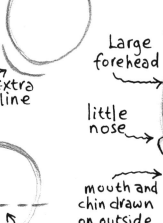

wispy hair

big head

thin neck

Then draw the whole head like this and rub out the pencil lines.

28

To draw cute baby animals you use much the same method as for drawing babies.

Keep the big eyes but this time draw a little triangle for the nose and mouth. Draw the head-shape next but this time make the cheeks chubbier.

Tall ears make it a baby rabbit.

Round ears make it a baby mouse.

Floppy ears make it a puppy.

Pointed ears make it a kitten.

When drawing a baby animal's body, use the same rules as for drawing a baby... except give the baby animal big feet!

Not all baby animals are chubby, of course. Here are two that are cute because they are the opposite!

Foal

Short ears

long neck with hair

Big head

hairy tail

Long, spindly legs

little hooves

Fawn

Long neck— no hair

Long ears

shorter, thicker body than the foal's

Big head but smaller than the foal's

Short tail

Long, spindly legs

little cloven hooves

Cartoon Round-up

Cartoon Puzzles

And finally...when you have finished drawing... try these puzzles and test your brain!

What are these?

1

2

3

These two kings look the same... but there are six differences. Can you see what they are?

4

5

6